FOREWORD

The story of the Democratic Republic of the Congo is one of contradictions—a land of immeasurable wealth, yet home to staggering poverty. This dichotomy is no accident; it has been meticulously engineered through decades of exploitation, systemic corruption, and global complicity. This book seeks to unravel the layers of financial strategies—some calculated, others chaotic—that have perpetuated this cycle. As an observer, student, and advocate, I have studied these mechanisms not merely to expose them but to challenge the narratives that bind the DRC to its troubled history. My hope is that this book serves as a resource for understanding, a tool for advocacy, and a spark for meaningful change.

FINANCIAL MACHIAVELLIANISM IN THE DEMOCRATIC REPUBLIC OF CONGO

WEST ORNAN MONGA

notionpress.com

INDIA · SINGAPORE · MALAYSIA

ISBN 979-8-89632-340-2

CONTENTS

PREFACE

The Democratic Republic of Congo (DRC) is a nation of immense potential, endowed with unparalleled natural resources and a vibrant population. Yet, its history has been marked by complex political, economic, and social challenges that have hindered its development and shaped its trajectory. At the heart of these challenges lies the phenomenon of financial Machiavellianism, strategic manipulation of public finances by political elites for personal or political gain, often at the expense of the nation's prosperity.

This book seeks to unravel the intricate web of financial Machiavellianism in the DRC, tracing its historical roots, analyzing its contemporary manifestations, and exploring the profound impact it has had on the country's governance, economy, and society. By delving into critical themes such as monetary and fiscal policies, the role of foreign influence, the exploitation of natural resources, and the participation of civil society, this work aims to provide a comprehensive understanding of how financial Machiavellianism operates and perpetuates itself in the DRC.

The chapters are not only a reflection of past and present realities but also a call to action. They challenge policymakers, scholars, civil society, and international stakeholders to rethink the governance structures and economic systems that enable such practices. Through critical analysis, the book identifies pathways for reform, emphasizing the importance of institutional strengthening, transparency, accountability, and civic engagement in fostering sustainable development.

This book is written not just as a scholarly endeavor but as a tribute to the resilience of the Congolese people, who continue to strive for a brighter future despite systemic challenges. It is a testament to their enduring hope for a nation where resources are managed equitably, governance is conducted ethically, and opportunities are accessible to all.

It is my hope that this work will serve as a resource for those seeking to understand the dynamics of financial governance in the DRC and as a guide for envisioning and building a more just, transparent, and prosperous future.

WEST ORNAN MONGA
Author

PROLOGUE

Nestled at the heart of Africa, the Democratic Republic of the Congo boasts unparalleled natural resources: vast forests, fertile soil, and mineral riches that have powered industries across the globe. Yet, the Congolese people have seen little of the prosperity such wealth should bring. Instead, they are often trapped in a web of foreign manipulation, domestic inefficiencies, and systemic corruption that has turned their blessings into burdens.

This book explores the financial underpinnings of this paradox, tracing how policies—both external and internal—have eroded trust and stifled growth. It uncovers the Machiavellian schemes that prioritize power over people, wealth over welfare, and short-term gains over long-term stability.

This is not just a critique; it is a call to action. The DRC's story is still being written, and its people remain resilient. The choices we make today can reshape the nation's destiny, building a future where resources are tools of empowerment, not exploitation.

Chapter 1

EMERGENCE

The State, as the founding institution of social order and collective security, stands as the guarantor of legal freedoms, defining citizens' rights and duties. Yet behind this protective appearance, a question remains: to what extent does the State truly respect individual freedoms when its financial and political interests are at stake?

The notion of legal freedom, though fundamentally noble, often finds itself at odds with the interests of the powerful. In the context of The Democratic Republic of Congo, where foreign influences and economic interests frequently dominate political decisions, legal freedom becomes an adjustable variable, manipulated according to the needs of those who hold power.

The Origin of the State and the Promise of Freedom

At the foundation of any organized society, the State was conceived as a social contract, a promise of regulated order in exchange for certain concessions made by individuals. However, this concept of the State as the guarantor of rights and freedoms has faced the realities of power, particularly in societies where resource exploitation and economic interests prevail. In the DRC, a country rich in natural resources but economically fragile, the State sometimes oscillates between the role of protector and regulator of freedoms, adjusting these to maintain stability, often threatened by political and economic crises.

The promise of legal freedom for all, theoretically inalienable, is often compromised when the state's financial interests and external actors interfere. Laws and regulations are shaped to secure economic agreements, sometimes at the expense of citizens' rights, transforming the promise of equality into an illusion.

Legal Freedom: An Instrument of Power and Control

In a state influenced by financial Machiavellianism, legal freedom becomes more than a mere guarantee of rights: it transforms into a strategic tool. Laws meant to protect citizens are often reinterpreted, even modified, to favor lucrative economic alliances. Access to justice becomes a privilege reserved for those who can exploit it politically or financially.

In the DRC, the reality is such that citizens' rights, while codified, are subject to the influence of international capital flows. Freedom of expression, property, and justice are, so to speak, 'negotiable' when they conflict with foreign investment projects or commercial interests. Thus, legal freedom loses substance and becomes a facade to justify decisions already made behind the scenes of economic agreements.

Foreign Influences: An Invisible Hand Shaping Freedom

In the DRC, foreign interests play a prominent role. The state finds itself in a position of financial dependency on international partners, leading it to adjust legislation to align local standards with these partners' requirements. This foreign influence results in restrictions on citizens' freedoms under the guise of economic development.

Investors and multinationals, primarily attracted by the country's mineral wealth, often impose exploitative conditions beyond local criticism. In exchange for financial concessions, the state limits opposition, protest, or regulatory rights of the population. These strategic alliances illustrate economic Machiavellianism, where legal freedom is subordinated to priorities of growth and profitability.

The Paradox of Freedom and Security

The State, justifying its actions in the name of security and general welfare, creates a paradox. While claiming to guarantee legal freedom, it controls it to prevent any form of dissent that might disrupt the established order. Thus, citizens become subjects of a regime that limits their rights, not to protect them but to maintain an appearance of stability essential to pursuing financial interests.

In the DRC, the fight against protest movements, restrictive laws on public demonstrations, and increased surveillance of civil society reveal this delicate balance. National security, invoked to restrict certain freedoms, often masks a desire to preserve acquired economic interests, contradicting the theoretically advocated legal freedom.

Toward Emancipation or an Illusion of Freedom?

The central question remains: is legal freedom, as promised to the citizens of the DRC, truly accessible? Or is it a carefully maintained illusion where the appearance of rights hides economic and political realities beyond the majority's control?

The emergence of the State as a guarantor of legal freedom, while working for its own economic survival, reveals a disturbing truth. In the play of financial influences and power, freedom is no longer a fundamental right but an adjustable variable. For the State, the primary goal is not so much the protection of its citizens but rather the preservation of its financial balance, often at the expense of legal equality.

In this analysis, it becomes clear that legal freedom in the DRC is inextricably linked to external economic forces and the interests of a privileged elite. Citizens, though seemingly free, remain hostages of a power structure that subtly manipulates the rights it is supposed to guarantee for its own survival.

This chapter develops the idea that the state, despite its theoretical role as a protector of freedoms, is influenced by financial and strategic imperatives, particularly in the DRC. Legal freedom thus becomes a tool of power, adjusted according to economic interests, creating a reality where the promise of equality remains an illusion for the majority of citizens.

CHAPTER 2

THE INITIATORS OF MACHIAVELLI

While history has remembered Niccolò Machiavelli as the architect of unscrupulous politics, it is clear that Machiavelli did not invent these power strategies. *The Prince*, his emblematic work, merely put into words a much older practice, one of cunning and manipulation in the service of regime stability and survival. But who are the true initiators of Machiavellian ideas, those historical and contemporary figures who laid the foundations of political philosophy where the end justifies the means?

The Principles of Machiavelli: Cunning, Power, and Pragmatism

Before exploring the initiators of this thought, it is essential to understand what the Machiavellian approach represents. In *The Prince*, Machiavelli describes a leader who must be pragmatic, flexible, and sometimes ruthless. This is not about morality but about power. Loyalty, virtue, and integrity are secondary if they hinder the effectiveness and survival of the State. The prince, for Machiavelli, must know how to conceal his intentions, manipulate perceptions, and even betray if necessary, for the ultimate goal is the preservation of his power.

The Precursors of Machiavellian Ideas

Long before Machiavelli, history reveals figures who already embodied these principles. Cesare Borgia, whom Machiavelli himself admired, is a striking example. To secure his authority, Borgia did not hesitate to use force, cunning, and even assassination, seeing these means as justifiable solutions to unify his territories. Alexander the Great, during his campaigns of conquest, also used tactics of manipulation, recruiting and reintegrating local elites to stabilize his empire. These historical figures demonstrate that the thirst for power and pragmatism already surpassed morality, thus establishing the foundations of Machiavellian thought.

From the Roman Empire to medieval kingdoms, leaders and rulers who marked history often acted in calculated ways, sacrificing ethics on the altar of efficiency. These initiators of Machiavelli, even without bearing the name, demonstrated that ambition and power go hand in hand with cunning and manipulation, a vision that resonates far beyond the pages written by the Florentine thinker.

Extending Machiavellian Principles to the Economy

Machiavellian thought has influenced not only politics; it has also permeated the workings of the economy. In a world where profit has become the ultimate goal, Machiavelli's principles find fertile ground. Large colonial companies, like the East India Company, used calculated methods to maximize their gains, not hesitating to use force, corruption, and exploitation of local populations to establish their economic dominance. They demonstrated that the economy could also become a field of power where cunning and manipulation are essential for maintaining lasting control.

This Machiavellian approach is present today in multinationals and economic elites, who wield immense influence over political decisions and the natural resources of many countries, particularly in Africa. In The Democratic Republic of Congo, this intrusion of economic Machiavellianism is palpable. The country's wealth attracts foreign interests, and Machiavelli's principles take on a new dimension, that of economic supremacy over national sovereignty.

Machiavellian Actors in the DRC

In the context of the DRC, local political and economic figures, often influenced by foreign interests, also adopt a Machiavellian approach. To secure their positions, leaders sometimes find themselves forced to negotiate opaque alliances or even restrict certain public freedoms to protect their own interests and those of their foreign partners. Machiavellian principles thus become a tool for management and control.

Congolese elites, in partnership with multinational corporations, exploit the country's resources, sometimes at the expense of the population. Laws are adjusted, the opposition is silenced, and resources are channeled to those who benefit the most. These actors, like Machiavelli's initiators, manipulate power structures to ensure apparent stability, leaving little room for the rights and interests of ordinary citizens.

The Legacy of the Initiators: An Ethic of Manipulation

The initiators of Machiavelli, whether ancient or modern, have left a complex legacy. In the DRC, this legacy manifests in an environment where the State and external financial interests share power. Legal freedom, social justice, and citizens' well-being are subordinated to a Machiavellian vision of power and efficiency. This cold pragmatism, which justifies all actions by maintaining economic and political authority, leaves little room for ethics and universal values of justice.

Machiavellian principles continue to dominate Congolese politics and the economy, creating a reality where citizens are often spectators of an opaque power game. In the end, the legacy of Machiavelli's initiators endures, and the DRC suffers the consequences, with restricted civil rights and an economy where manipulation is the rule rather than the exception.

CHAPTER 3

THE ERA OF INDEPENDENCE AND INITIAL DEVIATIONS

Introduction

This chapter explores the post-independence period in The Democratic Republic of Congo (DRC) and the first deviations from the ideals of economic autonomy and good governance. We will examine how initial hopes for fair and equitable economic management were diverted, leading to the emergence of Machiavellian financial practices with lasting impacts on the country.

Political and Economic Context After Independence

In 1960, the DRC gained independence, an event that sparked great hope and a sense of national renewal. However, the country quickly faced serious challenges.

Although rich in natural resources, the DRC lacked strong infrastructure and qualified human capital, making the management of the transition complex on both political and economic fronts.

1. **Transition from Colonial to National Governance**

The shift from colonial governance to national governance was marked by deep political instability. The administrative and economic structures inherited from colonization were insufficient to manage such a vast and diverse country.

The first Congolese leaders, including Patrice Lumumba, sought to implement economic policies aimed at rebuilding the economy and using natural resources for national development. However, these initiatives were often hindered by internal political conflicts and external interference.

2. **Conflicts and Secessions**

Shortly after independence, the DRC was plunged into a series of internal conflicts, including the secession of Katanga province. These conflicts weakened the central government and created an environment favorable to corruption and mismanagement of resources.

The First Deviations from Economic Ideals

1. **The Elimination of Patrice Lumumba**

Patrice Lumumba, an iconic figure of independence, advocated for genuine economic autonomy and the nationalization of resources for the benefit of all Congolese people. His elimination marked the beginning of a period where the ideals of social and economic justice were gradually eroded.

2. The Rise of Mobutu Sese Seko

In 1965, Mobutu Sese Seko took power, establishing an autocratic regime. He implemented economic policies that often favored personal enrichment and the consolidation of power over national development. The nationalization of foreign businesses initially intended to redistribute wealth, was diverted to serve a narrow elite.

3. Zairianization and Radicalization Policies

The 'Zairianization' and 'radicalization' policies of the 1970s aimed to transfer foreign businesses and properties to Congolese citizens. Although these measures were well-intentioned, their execution was flawed, leading to corruption and inefficient management. Many nationalized companies were assigned to regime allies who lacked the necessary skills to manage them, leading to their decline.

Economic and Social Impact

1. Collapse of Economic Institutions

The first deviations severely weakened economic institutions. The National Bank of Congo and other financial institutions were politicized, and economic decisions were often made for political rather than economic reasons.

The lack of transparency and accountability allowed corruption to thrive. Public resources were often diverted to enrich leaders and their close associates, leaving few means for investment in infrastructure and public services.

2. Deterioration of Living Conditions

Deviant economic practices had a direct impact on the quality of life for Congolese citizens. Essential public services, such as health, education, and infrastructure, were neglected. Economic inequalities widened, with a wealthy elite contrasting sharply with the majority of the population living in poverty.

The country's natural wealth, which could have been used to improve the lives of the population, was exploited in unsustainable and often illegal ways. The mining sector, in particular, was marked by illegal exploitation and forced labor, exacerbating conflicts and instability in mining regions.

International Actors and Their Influence

1. Foreign Interference

Foreign powers, notably the United States, the Soviet Union, and Belgium, played crucial roles in the early years of the DRC's independence. Often driven by geopolitical and economic interests, these interventions contributed to the country's destabilization.

These interferences supported certain regimes and groups at the expense of others, fueling internal conflicts and political rivalries. This dynamic complicated the implementation of stable and transparent economic policies.

2. Impact of International Financial Institutions

International financial institutions, such as the International Monetary Fund (IMF) and the World Bank, also influenced the economic policies of the DRC. Structural adjustment programs imposed in the 1980s and 1990s often demanded drastic economic reforms that had mixed effects on the Congolese economy.

Although these programs aimed to stabilize the economy and attract foreign investments, they often resulted in cuts to social spending and controversial privatizations, increasing the economic vulnerability of the population.

CHAPTER 4

THE FIRST FINANCIAL STRATEGIES

Introduction

This chapter analyses the initial financial strategies implemented in The Democratic Republic of Congo (DRC) after independence. We will examine how these strategies were designed, applied, and their effects on the Congolese economy and society.

We will also explore how these early approaches have influenced current financial practices.

Historical Context

After gaining independence from Belgium in 1960, the DRC faced complex economic and social challenges. Although endowed with abundant natural resources, the country lacked a solid economic structure and an effective public administration.

The early governments had to develop strategies to manage resources and stabilize the emerging economy.

The First Financial Policies

1. Nationalization of Natural Resources

Among the first measures taken after independence, the nationalization of natural resources was essential. This policy aimed to ensure that the country's wealth would directly benefit the Congolese population rather than foreign interests. However, this initiative was marred by major administrative challenges and allegations of corruption.

2. Creation of National Banks and Financial Institutions

The government established national financial institutions to regulate the economy. The National Bank of Congo (BNC) was created to manage monetary policy. Nevertheless, the lack of technical expertise and political interference compromised the effectiveness of these new institutions.

3. Development Programs and Infrastructure Projects

Ambitious development programs were launched to modernize the country, including the construction of roads, bridges, and electrical networks. These projects, primarily funded by international loans, led to significant debt, posing a major challenge to the Congolese economy.

Problems and Challenges

1. Corruption and Embezzlement of Funds

Corruption quickly became a central issue, with development funds frequently diverted by officials and political elites. This slowed economic progress and established a culture of financial misconduct.

2. **Lack of Transparency and Effective Management**

Public finance management suffered from a lack of transparency, with few accountability mechanisms. This opacity allowed dishonest practices to thrive, often without repercussions for those responsible.

3. **Dependence on Natural Resources**

The DRC became overly dependent on its natural resources without diversifying its economy. This made the country vulnerable to fluctuations in global commodity prices, and revenues from mineral exports were not reinvested in other economic sectors, creating an imbalanced economy.

The First Figures in Congolese Finance

1. **Patrice Lumumba and His Ideals**

Patrice Lumumba, the first Prime Minister of the DRC, embodied a vision of economic independence and social justice for Congo. Although his tenure was brief, his ideals left a lasting mark on the country's early economic policies.

2. **Mobutu Sese Seko and Kleptocracy**

Mobutu Sese Seko, an influential leader, profoundly impacted the DRC's early financial strategies. Under his regime, the country became a kleptocracy, where state resources were exploited to enrich the ruling elite. The financial strategies adopted under Mobutu primarily aimed to consolidate his personal power and enrich his supporters.

3. Long-term Consequences

The initial financial strategies implemented after independence had lasting effects on the Congolese economy. The practices established during this period contributed to the foundation of a financial Machiavellianism that persists today. The weakness of financial institutions, the culture of corruption, and the excessive dependence on natural resources have hindered the country's sustainable economic development.

CHAPTER 5

GOVERNING THROUGH LAWS AND FORCE

Introduction

The Democratic Republic of Congo (DRC) has undergone phases of dictatorship that have profoundly influenced its political and economic structures. These authoritarian regimes often facilitated the rise of shadow finance, creating an environment ripe for corruption and illicit financial practices. This chapter examines how these dictatorships promoted the growth of shadow finance, highlighting the methods used, the main actors involved, and the repercussions on Congolese society.

Historical and Political Context

Since its independence in 1960, the DRC has experienced several authoritarian regimes, with Mobutu Sese Seko being one of the most prominent figures. His reign, from 1965 to 1997, was characterized by the centralization of power and endemic corruption. Under his governance, democratic institutions were weakened, and national resources were captured by a small elite.

After Mobutu, although new leaders promised reforms, shadow finance practices often continued. Political instability and armed conflicts exacerbated economic challenges, creating fertile ground for corruption and illicit transactions.

Mechanisms of Shadow Finance

Shadow finance in the DRC manifests through practices such as money laundering, corruption, and embezzlement of public funds. These practices became institutionalized under dictatorship, protected by powerful influence networks.

Money Laundering

Money laundering, which involves legitimizing funds from illegal sources, is common in the DRC. Elites use offshore structures, shell companies, and complex transactions to disguise these financial flows. These methods allow profits from corruption and the exploitation of natural resources to be transformed into seemingly legal assets.

Corruption and Embezzlement of Funds

Corruption is pervasive in the public sector in the DRC, with poorly paid officials often resorting to bribes to supplement their income. Public funds intended for development are regularly diverted to finance personal projects or support political interests.

Case Studies and Specific Examples

- **The Case of Gécamines**

  Gécamines, a state-owned mining company, has long been at the center of corruption scandals. Under Mobutu, mining revenues were funneled into private accounts abroad, depriving the country of essential resources for its development.

Even after the regime ended, these opaque practices persisted, with millions of dollars regularly disappearing from the company's coffers.

- **The Case of Tenke Fungurume Mining (TFM)**

TFM is a joint venture between the state-owned Gécamines and foreign partners like Freeport-McMoRan and China Molybdenum Co., Ltd. Reports from the organization Global Witness raised concerns about the transparency of transactions between Gécamines and its private partners, particularly regarding the sale of mining assets at below-market prices.

Source: Global Witness, "Regime Cash Machine" (2017)

- **The Case of Katanga Mining**

This subsidiary of Glencore, a Swiss multinational, has been involved in corruption scandals and allegations of mismanagement. Glencore has been accused of bribing officials and signing opaque contracts with entities linked to influential businessmen, such as Dan Gertler, to secure mining concessions.

Source: Reuters, "Glencore faces bribery probe over Congo deals" (2018)

- **Dan Gertler Case**

Dan Gertler, an Israeli businessman, became a major player in the Congolese mining sector, notably through partnerships with Gécamines and other state-owned companies. He was accused by the U.S. government of using corruption to obtain mining contracts at preferential prices, leading to sanctions against him.

Source: U.S. Department of the Treasury, "Treasury Sanctions Fourteen Entities Affiliated with Corrupt Businessman Dan Gertler Under Global Magnitsky" (2017)

Social and Economic Consequences

Shadow finance has disastrous consequences for Congolese society. Systemic corruption and embezzlement of public funds deprive citizens of essential services such as healthcare, education, and infrastructure. Consequently, poverty and inequality persist despite the country's abundant natural resources.

Public institutions are weakened by shadow finance, compromising their ability to govern effectively. Public trust in institutions is eroded, worsening political and economic instability.

Efforts to Combat and Resilience

Despite these challenges, initiatives are underway to combat shadow finance in the DRC. Legislative reforms have been adopted to strengthen transparency and financial accountability. For example, the Extractive Industries Transparency Initiative (EITI) seeks to improve transparency in the extractive sector.

Non-governmental organizations and journalists play a key role in exposing abuses and advocating for reform. Whistleblowers, often at risk, help reveal illicit practices and raise public awareness.

Perspectives and Reflections

To overcome the challenges posed by shadow finance, the DRC requires deep and sustained reforms. Strengthening the rule of law, promoting transparency, and holding leaders accountable are crucial steps. The international community also has a role to play by supporting local initiatives and imposing sanctions on corrupt actors.

The future of the DRC will depend on its ability to establish a fair and transparent financial system that serves the entire population rather than a privileged minority. This will require continuous commitment and strong political will to break away from past practices.

CHAPTER 6

POWER DYNAMICS, RIVALRIES, AND CONQUESTS

Introduction

The years of crisis in The Democratic Republic of Congo (DRC) have been marked by persistent armed conflicts and chronic political instability. These turbulent periods have had devastating economic impacts but also demonstrated the resilience of certain segments of society, particularly the political elites. This chapter explores the economic impacts of armed conflicts and the economic survival strategies adopted by political elites to maintain and consolidate their power.

Economic Impacts of Armed Conflicts

Since the fall of Mobutu Sese Seko in 1997, the DRC has experienced a series of armed conflicts that have ravaged the country. The First Congo War (1996–1997) and the Second Congo War (1998–2003), often called the 'African World War' due to the involvement of several African countries, deeply affected the Congolese economy.

Destruction of Infrastructure

Armed conflicts have led to massive destruction of infrastructure. Roads, bridges, schools, and hospitals have been damaged or destroyed, hindering the movement of goods and people and limiting access to essential services. The degradation of infrastructure has also impacted the mining sector, a pillar of the Congolese economy, making it difficult to extract and export natural resources.

For example, the railway network, essential for transporting minerals from Katanga to ports, was severely damaged. Destroyed bridges and impassable roads isolated mineral-producing regions, further complicating the export of these resources.

Collapse of the Economic Fabric

The fighting disrupted local economic activities. Farmers were forced to abandon their land, leading to a drop in agricultural production and worsening food insecurity. Many businesses closed or scaled down operations, resulting in increased unemployment and poverty. In conflict zones, local markets were often looted and destroyed, leading to shortages of basic consumer goods and rising prices. Small and medium-sized businesses were particularly affected, suffering significant financial losses and widespread closures.

Population Exodus

The conflicts triggered massive population displacements. Millions of people were internally displaced or fled to neighboring countries, creating a large-scale humanitarian crisis. These displacements not only disrupted local communities but also placed additional strain on already fragile local economies.

Refugee camps and host communities often lacked resources to cope with the massive influx of displaced people. Health and education infrastructure were overwhelmed, and living conditions in camps were often precarious, with limited access to clean water and food.

Corruption and War Economy

The conflicts also fostered the emergence of a war economy. Armed groups and criminal networks took control of resource-rich areas, illegally exploiting diamond, gold, and coltan mines to fund their activities. This illegal exploitation deprived the state of essential revenues and fueled corruption and violence.

Conflict minerals, like coltan used in electronic devices, were extracted under deplorable conditions and sold on the international market by armed groups. The profits from these sales were used to purchase weapons and finance military operations, prolonging conflicts and the suffering of local populations.

Economic Survival Strategies of Political Elites

In the face of this crisis, the DRC's political elites deployed various strategies to ensure their economic survival and maintain their power. These strategies often involved exploiting natural resources, manipulating state institutions, and forming tactical alliances.

Manipulation of State Institutions

Elites also manipulated state institutions to consolidate their power and protect their economic interests. This included appointing allies to key positions, influencing the judicial system to avoid prosecution for corruption, and using security forces to suppress opposition and maintain order.

Elections in the DRC have often been marred by fraud and irregularities, allowing elites to retain power. Oversight institutions, such as the Court of Auditors and anti-corruption agencies, have been systematically weakened or co-opted, making reform and transparency efforts difficult.

Tactical Alliances

During crises, tactical alliances with national and international actors were crucial. Political elites often formed alliances with armed groups, traditional leaders, and foreign partners to reinforce their power. These alliances, although often unstable, allowed elites to navigate through periods of turbulence.

For example, during conflicts, some elites partnered with armed groups to secure mining areas and ensure resource exports. Internationally, alliances with foreign powers provided political and financial support in exchange for economic concessions.

Diversification of Revenue Sources

To minimize risks, elites diversified their revenue sources by investing in various economic sectors such as real estate, trade, and services. These investments provided them with financial security and reduced their dependence on natural resource revenues.

Urban centers like Kinshasa and Lubumbashi experienced rapid real estate growth, often funded by capital from corruption and embezzlement. These real estate investments created pockets of wealth in a general context of poverty, highlighting the economic inequality exacerbated by the crises.

Conclusion

The years of crisis in the DRC have had devastating economic impacts, but they have also revealed the resilience and adaptability of political elites. By exploiting natural resources, manipulating state institutions, and forging tactical alliances, these elites managed to maintain their power and survive economically in an unstable environment. However, these strategies were often implemented at the expense of the Congolese population, exacerbating poverty, corruption, and instability.

CHAPTER 7

MACHIAVELLIAN REALISM: CONFLICT AT THE HEART OF POLITICS IN THE DRC

Introduction

Globalization has profoundly transformed the global economy, and The Democratic Republic of Congo (DRC) has not been spared by these changes. While it has offered opportunities for growth and development, globalization has also created complex side effects. This chapter explores the influence of multinational corporations and international financial institutions on the Congolese economy, as well as the new forms of financial Machiavellianism that have emerged in the era of globalization.

The Influence of Multinationals and International Financial Institutions

- **Multinationals in the DRC:** Multinational corporations hold a significant position in the DRC's economy, especially in the mining sector. Companies such as Glencore, China Molybdenum, and Ivanhoe Mines have invested heavily in extracting the country's natural resources, exploiting its rich deposits of copper, cobalt, and coltan.

Although these investments have brought economic benefits, such as job creation and tax revenues for the state, they have also presented major challenges:

- **Resource Exploitation**: Multinationals are often accused of exploiting the DRC's natural resources without ensuring a fair distribution of benefits. Mining contracts often lack transparency and are negotiated in ways that favor companies over the Congolese state.

- **International Financial Institutions:** International financial institutions, such as the International Monetary Fund (IMF) and the World Bank, also exert significant influence over the Congolese economy. Their loans and reform programs aim to stabilize the economy and promote development, but these interventions are often controversial.

- **Working Conditions:** Working conditions in mines controlled by multinationals are often precarious, with low wages and inadequate safety. Human rights violations, such as child labor, are also commonly reported.

- **Environmental Impact:** Large-scale mining has serious environmental consequences, such as deforestation, water pollution, and the destruction of natural habitats. These impacts severely affect local communities who depend on these ecosystems for their livelihood. International Financial Institutions International financial institutions, such as the International Monetary Fund (IMF) and the World Bank, also exert significant influence over the Congolese economy. Their loans and reform programs aim to stabilize the economy and promote development, but these interventions are often controversial.

- **Structural Adjustment Programs**: In the 1980s and 1990s, the DRC adopted structural adjustment programs under the supervision of the IMF and the World Bank. These programs imposed austerity measures, such as reducing public spending, privatizing state-owned enterprises, and liberalizing markets. While some reforms were necessary, they also led to mass layoffs, increased poverty, and a deterioration of public services.

- **Loan Conditionality**: Loans from international financial institutions often come with strict conditions that limit the DRC's economic sovereignty. These conditions may include fiscal reforms, subsidy cuts, and deregulation policies, which do not always consider local realities and may exacerbate inequalities.

- **Transparency and Accountability**: Efforts by international financial institutions to promote transparency and good governance in the DRC are essential, but the results are mixed. Corruption and misappropriation of funds remain major issues, limiting the effectiveness of international aid and development programs.

New Forms of Financial Machiavellianism in the Era of Globalization

Globalization has also given rise to sophisticated forms of financial Machiavellianism, where economic and political actors use complex strategies to maximize their power and profits. These practices include tax evasion, the use of tax havens, and financial market manipulation.

Tax Evasion and Tax Havens

Tax evasion has become a common practice among the political and economic elites of the DRC. Through offshore structures and tax havens, these actors can conceal their income and avoid paying taxes in their home country.

- **Tax Evasion Techniques:** Multinationals and Congolese elites use sophisticated techniques like transfer pricing, where companies manipulate the prices of goods and services exchanged between their subsidiaries in different countries to reduce their taxable income.

- **Tax Havens:** Tax havens offer attractive tax advantages and financial confidentiality, allowing individuals and companies to hide their assets.

- Jurisdictions such as the Cayman Islands, Luxembourg, and Switzerland are commonly used for this purpose.

Financial Market Manipulation

Globalization has also allowed powerful actors to manipulate financial markets. By using insider information, speculative practices, and complex investment strategies, these actors can influence asset prices and make substantial profits.

- **Insider Trading:** The use of non-public information to conduct transactions in financial markets is illegal but difficult to detect and prove. In the DRC, connections between political elites and financial markets create opportunities for such practices.

- **Commodity Speculation:** The DRC's wealth in natural resources makes its commodities targets for speculation by financial actors. This speculation can lead to price fluctuations that impact the national economy and revenue stability.

Transnational Corruption

Globalization also facilitates transnational corruption, where foreign companies and governments engage in corrupt practices to secure lucrative contracts and agreements.

- **Corruption in Mining Contracts:** Multinational companies have been accused of paying bribes to Congolese officials to secure profitable mining contracts. These practices undermine governance and deprive the state of legitimate revenue.

- **Money Laundering:** Illicit financial flows from corruption, tax evasion, and illegal resource exploitation are often laundered through complex transactions and international financial networks. Money laundering allows these funds to be reintegrated into the legal economy, masking their criminal origins.

Conclusion

Globalization has brought both opportunities and challenges to the DRC. The influence of multinationals and international financial institutions has been significant yet often ambiguous, providing economic benefits alongside negative side effects. In the era of globalization, new forms of financial Machiavellianism have developed, exacerbating inequalities and corruption.

To navigate this complex global landscape, the DRC must undertake structural reforms, adopt more transparent governance, and strengthen international cooperation. Combating tax evasion, financial market manipulation, and transnational corruption is crucial to ensure equitable and sustainable development.

Ultimately, it is essential that the benefits of globalization are fairly distributed to improve the living conditions of all Congolese, not just the privileged elite.

CHAPTER 8

INSTITUTIONAL AND LEGAL RESPONSES

Introduction

In response to corruption and financial scandals, The Democratic Republic of Congo (DRC) has implemented various institutional and legal measures to regulate and reform its system. This chapter explores initiatives aimed at combating corruption, as well as the successes and failures of anti-corruption policies.

- Efforts at Regulation and Reform

- Creation of Anti-Corruption Institutions

The DRC has established several institutions to fight corruption and promote transparency:

- National Anti-Corruption Commission (CNLCC): This commission coordinates anti-corruption efforts, investigates suspicious cases, promotes transparency within public institutions, and raises public awareness.

- Corruption and Professional Ethics Monitoring Observatory (OSCEP): OSCEP monitors ethical practices in both public and private sectors, collects complaints, and proposes reforms to improve ethics.

Legislative and Regulatory Reforms

The Congolese government has introduced several reforms to strengthen anti-corruption efforts and improve governance:

- Law on Money Laundering and Terrorist Financing (2018): This law aims to prevent money laundering and terrorist financing by strengthening reporting obligations for financial institutions and imposing strict sanctions.

- Law on Transparency and Governance in the Natural Resources Sector (2015): This law mandates public disclosure of mining and petroleum contracts and requires companies to publish payments made to authorities.

- Revised Mining Code (2018): The updated mining code introduced measures to increase royalties, strengthen environmental and social requirements, and improve transparency in license allocations.

International Initiatives and Partnerships

The DRC participates in several international initiatives to promote transparency and combat corruption:

- Extractive Industries Transparency Initiative (EITI): As a member of EITI, the DRC commits to publishing revenues from natural resources and improving citizen participation in the governance of the extractive sectors.

- Partnerships with International Organizations: The DRC collaborates with the World Bank, IMF, and European Union to implement institutional reforms and build capacity.

Successes and Failures of Anti-Corruption Policies

Successes

Some anti-corruption initiatives in the DRC have yielded positive results:

- Improved Transparency: Membership in EITI has led to greater transparency in the extractive sector, with reports detailing company payments and state revenues, facilitating oversight by civil society.

- Empowerment of Civil Society: Reforms have strengthened the role of civil society organizations, such as the Coalition for Transparency and Governance of Natural Resources (CTGRN), in monitoring public policies and raising awareness.

Failures

However, several challenges persist:

- Lack of Political Will: The absence of commitment at the highest levels remains a major obstacle, with political and economic elites often involved in corruption having little incentive to support reforms that threaten their interests.

- Institutional Weakness: Anti-corruption institutions often lack resources and independence. Both the CNLCC and OSCEP suffer from underfunding and political interference, limiting their effectiveness.

- Impunity: A culture of impunity is deeply entrenched, with few prosecutions of corrupt officials and investigations often hindered by political pressures.

- Complexity and Slow Pace of Reforms: Reforms are often complex and slow to implement, with bureaucratic processes delaying progress.

Conclusion

The DRC's institutional and legal responses to corruption range from the creation of institutions to the implementation of legislative reforms and international partnerships. While some initiatives have improved transparency and strengthened civil society, many challenges remain. The lack of political will, institutional weaknesses, impunity, and slow reform processes continue to hinder anti-corruption efforts.

To effectively combat corruption, it is essential to strengthen governance institutions, ensure the funding and independence of anti-corruption agencies, and foster a culture of transparency and accountability. International cooperation and civil society support are also crucial to ensuring that the DRC's resources benefit its entire population.

CHAPTER 9

THE ROLE OF CIVIL SOCIETY AND THE MEDIA

Introduction

The Democratic Republic of Congo (DRC) faces significant economic challenges, exacerbated by a history of colonization, dictatorships, and conflicts. Among these challenges, financial Machiavellianism, the exploitation and misappropriation of public funds by elites for personal gain, is particularly notable. In this context, civil society and the media play a vital role in combating these practices. By exposing corruption and raising public awareness, these actors become essential in promoting transparency and financial accountability. This chapter examines how these entities mobilize against the country's financial challenges.

Civil Society: Actors and Initiatives

Civil society in the DRC comprises a variety of NGOs, associations, and citizen movements dedicated to social and economic justice. These organizations are often at the forefront of denouncing financial misconduct and advocating for reforms.

NGOs and Their Roles

Local and international NGOs, such as the Congolese League Against Corruption (LICOCO) and Global Witness, play a crucial role in exposing financial scandals.

They conduct in-depth investigations and publish reports on the misappropriation of public funds and suspicious transactions. For instance, Global Witness uncovered how millions of dollars from mining resources were siphoned off by Congolese officials and foreign companies.

LICOCO focuses on corruption at a more local level, working with affected communities to gather evidence and put pressure on local authorities. These efforts are often accompanied by awareness campaigns to mobilize public opinion against corruption.

Citizen Movements

Movements like Lucha (Lutte pour le Changement) mobilize the population to demand greater transparency and accountability from leaders. They organize protests, awareness campaigns, and lobbying actions to influence public policy. For example, Lucha uses social media to mobilize large crowds and draw attention to issues of corruption and poor governance.

These movements often face government repression, but their determination and decentralized organization have been crucial in maintaining pressure on authorities.

Their use of modern technologies to coordinate actions is a key factor in their success.

The Media: Guardians of Transparency

Congolese media, despite numerous challenges, has played a pivotal role in uncovering questionable financial practices. They are often the primary channel through which information on corruption and financial abuses reaches the public.

Investigative Journalism

Investigative journalists working for outlets like RFI (Radio France Internationale) and local publications take significant risks in exposing corruption. Their reports highlight cases of embezzlement, money laundering, and illegal contracts. For example, investigations into mining and petroleum transactions have revealed how high-ranking officials used shell companies to siphon revenues from natural resources.

These journalists use anonymous sources, leaked documents, and sophisticated investigative techniques to uncover illegal practices, often collaborating with international NGOs to amplify the impact of their findings.

Challenges for the Media

Media in the DRC frequently face censorship, threats, and physical attacks. Despite these obstacles, they continue to play a critical role in informing the public and pressuring authorities for greater transparency.

Media owners may also be influenced by political and economic interests, which sometimes limit journalist's freedom. However, the rise of online media and social platforms has opened new avenues for disseminating information, allowing journalists to bypass some restrictions imposed by traditional media.

Synergies Between Civil Society and Media

Collaboration between civil society and the media is often crucial in combating financial Machiavellianism. NGOs provide data and evidence, while the media disseminates this information to a broad audience, maximizing its impact.

Awareness Campaigns

Joint campaigns, such as those targeting corruption in the mining sector, demonstrate how these two actors can work effectively together. By combining the in-depth research of NGOs with the media's reach, these campaigns highlight critical issues. For instance, a joint campaign by Global Witness and local media revealed how mining profits were diverted to offshore accounts, sparking international reactions and leading to official investigations.

Workshops and Training

Workshops and training sessions for journalists and civil society members strengthen this synergy. By sharing investigative techniques and reporting methods, these initiatives enhance the quality of corruption investigations. For example, programs funded by international organizations have trained young journalists and activists in investigative journalism and digital tools to document corruption.

These collaborations have also fostered networks of support and solidarity among journalists and activists, providing them with resources and protection against threats.

Case Studies and Impact

Several case studies illustrate the significant impact of civil society and the media in combating financial Machiavellianism in the DRC.

The Mining Contracts Scandal

One example is the mining contracts scandal uncovered by Global Witness and disseminated by various media outlets. This investigation exposed financial misappropriation in opaque transactions, leading to international pressure and government reforms. The revelations showed the complicity of high-ranking Congolese officials and foreign companies in diverting funds intended for development projects.

The Central Bank Scandal

Another case is the Central Bank of the DRC scandal, where public funds were embezzled. Revelations by local NGOs, amplified by the media, led to an official investigation and reforms aimed at strengthening financial governance. The investigations uncovered a complex network of illegal transactions involving officials and international financial institutions, resulting in prosecutions and financial reforms.

Conclusion

Civil society and the media play a crucial role in combating financial Machiavellianism in the DRC. Despite challenges and risks, these actors continue to fight for greater transparency and accountability. Their collaboration contributes to exposing financial abuses and fostering a culture of responsibility essential for the country's sustainable development. By strengthening their partnerships and capabilities, civil society and the media can become powerful catalysts for a more just and equitable DRC.

CHAPTER 10

PUBLIC-PRIVATE PARTNERSHIPS: OPPORTUNITIES AND CHALLENGES

Introduction

Public-Private Partnerships (PPPs) in The Democratic Republic of Congo (DRC) represent a strategic approach to fostering the country's economic and social development. By combining the resources and expertise of the private sector with the mission and objectives of the public sector, these collaborations can unlock critical resources for infrastructure and public service projects. However, these partnerships are not without risks, particularly in a context where corruption and favoritism remain significant challenges. This chapter explores the benefits and potential pitfalls of PPPs in the DRC, highlighting the conditions necessary to maximize their advantages while minimizing their risks.

Advantages of Public-Private Partnerships in the DRC

Mobilization of Financial Resources

In a country where public resources are often limited, PPPs provide a valuable opportunity to mobilize private capital for ambitious projects. For instance, in the infrastructure sector, PPPs enable the financing of roads, bridges, hospitals, and schools, projects that would otherwise be beyond the reach of public funding alone.

These partnerships are particularly beneficial for energy projects, such as hydroelectric or solar power plants, where initial investment costs are high.

Improved Operational Efficiency

Private enterprises, driven by profitability, are often more efficient in managing projects than public entities. They bring management practices focused on performance, efficiency, and timely delivery. This expertise can lead to cost reductions, improved service quality, and faster project completion. For example, in the healthcare sector, private management has sometimes provided higher-quality services at lower costs.

Technological Innovation

The private sector, often at the forefront of innovation, can introduce modern technologies and methods in public service management. This is especially true in sectors like water and sanitation, where advanced technological solutions can improve access to clean water and waste management. By integrating these innovations, PPPs can help modernize public services in the DRC, making them more efficient and sustainable.

Risk-Sharing

PPPs also allow for a redistribution of risks between public and private partners. By sharing financial, technical, and operational risks, these partnerships reduce the burden on the public sector while making projects more attractive to private investors. This risk-sharing is crucial for attracting private investment to long-term projects, which are often perceived as high risk.

Challenges of Public-Private Partnerships in the DRC

Corruption Risks

Corruption is a pervasive issue that can undermine the benefits of PPPs in the DRC.

Tendering and contract awarding processes are often vulnerable to manipulation, favoring companies that offer bribes or have political connections. These practices lead to cost overruns, delays, and substandard projects, eroding public and investor confidence. Strong governance mechanisms are essential to prevent corruption and ensure that projects genuinely serve public interests.

Favoritism

Favoritism is another problem that can compromise the effectiveness of PPPs in the DRC. Companies with close ties to political figures may be favored in contract awards, undermining competition and transparency. This favoritism discourages potential investors and can result in inefficient resource allocation, with priority projects neglected in favor of those benefiting influential individuals.

Lack of Transparency

A lack of transparency in PPP management is a significant barrier to its success.

When contract terms and selection processes are not open to the public, it becomes difficult for citizens and civil society organizations to monitor and evaluate project effectiveness. This lack of transparency increases the risk of corruption and abuse while undermining accountability among stakeholders.

Elite Capture of Benefits

Finally, there is a risk that the benefits of PPPs will be captured by elites at the expense of local populations. Projects may be designed to serve the private interests of a few rather than addressing the urgent needs of communities. This reflects a pattern of financial Machiavellianism, where public resources are diverted to benefit a minority, leaving the majority without access to essential services.

Conclusion

Public-private partnerships offer significant opportunities for the development of the DRC, particularly in the infrastructure and public service sectors. However, to ensure these partnerships are genuinely beneficial, it is essential to implement robust governance mechanisms focused on transparency, accountability, and anti-corruption efforts. By strengthening institutional capacities and encouraging citizen participation, the DRC can maximize the advantages of PPPs while minimizing the risks of misuse. Ethical and transparent management of PPPs is crucial to transforming these opportunities into tangible benefits for the Congolese population as a whole.

CHAPTER 11

MONETARY AND FISCAL POLICIES

Introduction

Monetary and fiscal policies are the primary tools through which governments aim to regulate the economy, stabilize prices, promote growth, and maintain financial stability. In The Democratic Republic of Congo (DRC), a country facing unique economic, political, and social challenges, these policies hold critical importance.

However, it is not uncommon for these policies to be misused for personal or political gain, exemplifying a form of financial Machiavellianism. This chapter delves into the nature and impact of monetary and fiscal policies in the DRC while also examining the Machiavellian strategies employed to influence their implementation.

Section 1: Monetary Policies in the DRC

Role of the Central Bank

The Central Bank of Congo (BCC) is the institution responsible for implementing monetary policy in the DRC. Its primary mission is to maintain price stability, ensure financial stability, and promote balanced economic growth. The BCC utilizes various tools to regulate the money supply, influence interest rates, and oversee the banking system.

In an economic environment often disrupted by external shocks, internal political instability, and fragile financial infrastructure, the BCC plays a crucial role. Managing monetary policy in such a context requires significant expertise and a deep understanding of both local and global economic dynamics.

Monetary Policy Tools

The key tools of the BCC's monetary policy include:

- Interest Rates: The BCC adjusts benchmark interest rates to influence borrowing costs and encourage or discourage savings. For instance, raising interest rates can curb inflation by making credit more expensive but may also slow economic growth by reducing investments.

- Reserve Requirements: The BCC may impose reserve requirements on commercial banks, limiting their ability to lend money and thus influencing the money supply. Increasing reserve requirements reduces liquidity available for loans, helping to control inflation.

- Open Market Operations: The BCC buys or sells securities to regulate liquidity.

- Buying securities injects money into the economy, while selling securities withdraws money, potentially reducing inflation.

- Foreign Exchange Market Intervention: The BCC can intervene in the foreign exchange market to stabilize the exchange rate. In a country like the DRC, which is heavily reliant on imports, exchange rate stability is critical.

Objectives and Challenges

The main objectives of monetary policy in the DRC include controlling inflation, stabilizing the exchange rate, and promoting sustainable economic growth.

However, achieving these objectives is complicated by several challenges:

- Volatile Inflation: Inflation in the DRC is influenced by external factors like commodity price fluctuations and internal factors such as political instability, making it difficult for the BCC to maintain stable monetary policy.

- Dollarization of the Economy: The widespread use of the U.S. dollar in domestic transactions limits the effectiveness of the BCC's monetary policies. Dollarization reduces the BCC's ability to directly control the national economy.

- Underdeveloped Financial Sector: The DRC's financial sector is still underdeveloped, limiting the impact of monetary policy as financial institutions often struggle to respond effectively to policy changes.

- Public Confidence: Trust in the financial system and the national currency has been eroded by periods of high inflation and financial crises. Restoring public confidence remains a constant challenge for the BCC.

Machiavellianism in Monetary Policy

Monetary policy in the DRC is not immune to Machiavellian manipulations. Influential economic actors, including politicians and elites, may leverage their power to sway the BCC's decisions to their advantage. These pressures can include manipulating interest rates to ease credit access for specific projects or stabilizing the exchange rate to protect the financial interests of powerful actors.

For example, foreign exchange interventions may be used to avert economic crises ahead of elections or stabilize the national currency to safeguard investments of political allies. Such manipulations can undermine the BCC's priorities and jeopardize long-term economic stability.

Section 2: Fiscal Policies in the DRC

Role of the Government

The Congolese government, through the Ministry of Finance, is responsible for formulating and implementing fiscal policy. This includes taxation, public spending, and debt management. The primary goal of fiscal policy is to mobilize resources to fund public services and infrastructure while ensuring an equitable distribution of wealth.

In the DRC, where development needs are immense, but resources are limited, fiscal policy is a critical tool for stimulating the economy and reducing inequality. However, its effectiveness is often compromised by structural and institutional challenges.

Fiscal Policy Tools

The main instruments of fiscal policy in the DRC include:

- **Direct and Indirect Taxes**: Direct taxes include income taxes on individuals and corporations, while indirect taxes encompass VAT, customs duties, and excise taxes. Direct taxes are generally more equitable as they are based on the ability to pay, while indirect taxes can be more regressive.

- **Public Expenditures**: The government invests in infrastructure projects, education, healthcare, and other social services. These expenditures can stimulate the economy by creating jobs and improving infrastructure but must be managed prudently to avoid excessive deficits.

- **Debt Management:** Effective management of public debt is essential for maintaining investor confidence and avoiding solvency crises. In the DRC, a well-designed debt management strategy is crucial to meet financing needs while avoiding debt traps.

Objectives and Challenges

Fiscal policy in the DRC aims to promote economic growth, reduce poverty, and maintain macroeconomic stability. However, it faces several challenges:

- **Tax Evasion and Fraud**: Tax evasion reduces public revenue, limiting the government's ability to fund essential services. Weak fiscal institutions and corruption exacerbate this issue.

- **Dependence on Natural Resources:** Reliance on revenue from natural resources exposes the budget to commodity price fluctuations, making budget planning difficult.

- **Limited Administrative Capacity:** Weak fiscal institutions and limited administrative capacity hinder the effective collection of taxes and management of public expenditures.

- **Regional Inequalities:** The DRC's vast territory and significant regional disparities require fiscal policy to address differences to ensure equitable resource and public service distribution.

Machiavellianism in Fiscal Policy

Fiscal policy in the DRC is also subject to Machiavellian influences. Economic and political elites may use their power to shape fiscal legislation to their advantage. This can include tax exemptions for companies affiliated with influential actors, public spending directed toward projects that benefit specific interests, and manipulation of debt management to serve short-term political goals.

For instance, tax reliefs may be granted to businesses owned by political allies, or infrastructure projects may be directed to specific regions based on political considerations rather than economic needs. Similarly, public debt management decisions may prioritize electoral objectives, such as maintaining high spending levels to gain electoral support, at the expense of long-term financial stability.

Conclusion

Monetary and fiscal policies are essential tools for economic management in the DRC. However, their effectiveness is often undermined by significant structural and institutional challenges. A deeper understanding of these policies and their impacts is crucial for designing strategies to improve economic stability and promote sustainable growth in the DRC.

By examining these policies through the lens of financial Machiavellianism, we can better understand the power dynamics and political considerations influencing economic decision-making in the country. Moving forward, it is critical for the DRC to strengthen its financial and fiscal institutions, enhance transparency and accountability in economic policy management, and actively combat Machiavellian practices that undermine equitable and sustainable economic development.

CHAPTER 12

THE IMPACT OF FOREIGN POLICIES

Introduction

The economic history of The Democratic Republic of Congo (DRC) is deeply shaped by the influence of foreign powers. From the colonial era to the present day, the geopolitical and economic interests of foreign nations have significantly impacted the country's economic policies, affecting both its development and sovereignty.

This chapter explores how these external influences manifest, the underlying motivations of the involved powers, and their consequences for the Congolese economy.

1. Strategic and Economic Interests

The DRC's vast natural wealth, particularly in strategic minerals such as cobalt, copper, coltan, and diamonds, has consistently drawn the attention of foreign powers. These resources are critical for global technological and energy industries, positioning the DRC as a key player on the international stage.

China

China has emerged as a major economic partner for the DRC over the past two decades. The 'resources for infrastructure' agreements are emblematic of this relationship. In exchange for mining concessions, China finances the construction of roads, hospitals, and other essential infrastructure.

Positive Impacts

- Debt Relief: Initiatives such as the Heavily Indebted Poor Countries (HIPC) program have reduced the DRC's financial burden.

- Project Financing: Loans have funded essential infrastructure and development projects.

Negative Impacts

- Strict Conditionalities: Debt restructuring plans often come with stringent conditions that restrict the country's economic sovereignty.

- Recurring Debt: Despite debt relief efforts, the DRC continues to accumulate debt, posing challenges for long-term economic sustainability.

2. Consequences of Foreign Influence

The influence of foreign powers on the DRC's economic policies presents significant opportunities and challenges.

Economic Sovereignty

The DRC's economic sovereignty is often compromised by foreign interference.

Crucial economic decisions are influenced by foreign partners, limiting the country's ability to implement autonomous policies.

Examples of Compromised Sovereignty

- **Loan Agreements**: Loan terms can impose severe restrictions on the country's economic policies.

- **Aid Conditionalities**: Reform requirements tied to aid may not align with local needs and priorities.

Challenges and Opportunities

To address the challenges of foreign influence, the DRC must adopt strategies to strengthen governance, diversify its economy, and reduce dependence on foreign powers.

Potential Strategies

- **Strengthening Governance:** Improving transparency and combating corruption to create a stable and attractive environment for both local and foreign investments.

- **Economic Diversification:** Promoting sectors beyond mining to reduce reliance on natural resources.

- **Balanced Partnerships:** Negotiating agreements that respect national sovereignty and maximize benefits for local populations.

Conclusion

The influence of foreign powers on the DRC's economic policies is a complex reality with multifaceted implications. While international investments and aid have brought significant benefits, they have also constrained economic sovereignty and posed challenges to sustainable development. The DRC must carefully navigate its international relationships, safeguarding its national interests while leveraging opportunities for economic growth and sustainable development. A balanced and strategic approach is essential to ensure a prosperous and independent future for the country.

Chapter 13

THE APEX OF FINANCIAL MACHIAVELLIANISM IN THE DRC

Introduction

The rise of financial Machiavellianism in the Democratic Republic of Congo (DRC) is deeply rooted in the country's political and economic history. This concept refers to the manipulation of public finances by elites to maintain and consolidate power, often at the expense of the country's economic development. This chapter examines the defining periods in Congolese history that contributed to the entrenchment and evolution of these practices and analyses the factors that led to the peak of financial Machiavellianism in the DRC.

1. Defining Historical Periods

The post-independence history of the DRC is characterized by periods of political and economic crises, during which financial Machiavellianism took root and intensified.

Post-Independence Period (1960s–1970s)

After gaining independence in 1960, the DRC plunged into an era of political instability marked by coups and internal conflicts. Mobutu Sese Seko's rise to power in 1965 ushered in a period of systemic corruption, where state resources were diverted to serve the personal interests of the ruling elite.

Mobutu Sese Seko's Rule (1965–1997)

Under Mobutu, the DRC was transformed into a full-fledged kleptocracy. State-owned enterprises were nationalized, enabling the regime to control the economy tightly and concentrate wealth in the hands of a select few. Mobutu strategically used public finances to consolidate his power, distributing wealth to loyalists and suppressing opposition.

Transition Period (1997–2001)

The fall of Mobutu and the ascension of Laurent-Désiré Kabila in 1997 did not mark the end of financial Machiavellianism. Instead, the subsequent civil war saw intensified corruption as armed groups and political actors exploited natural resources to fund their activities.

Joseph Kabila's Regime (2001–2019)

Joseph Kabila's regime failed to curb endemic corruption in the DRC. Despite announcing reforms to improve governance, the embezzlement of public funds and personal enrichment at the highest levels of the state remained rampant. This period solidified financial Machiavellianism within the political elite.

Current Situation

Since Félix Tshisekedi's election in 2019, anti-corruption reforms have been promised, but significant challenges persist. Corruption and embezzlement continue to plague the DRC, raising questions about whether the country has reached the zenith of financial Machiavellianism.

2. Factors Contributing to the Apex of Financial Machiavellianism

Several factors have driven the rise of financial Machiavellianism in the DRC, entrenching this phenomenon over decades.

Abundant Natural Resources

The DRC's immense mineral wealth, particularly in cobalt, copper, and diamonds, has been both a blessing and a curse. These resources have attracted the greed of political and economic elites who exploit them for personal gain, often at the expense of national development.

Weak Institutions

Governance institutions in the DRC are often weak and susceptible to corruption.

This institutional fragility allows elites to embezzle public funds with impunity, perpetuating the cycle of corruption.

Conflict and Instability

Periods of conflict have exacerbated financial Machiavellian practices. Military and political factions have sought to enrich themselves by exploiting natural resources to fund their activities, further deepening the country's economic and social crises.

Lack of Transparency and Accountability

The lack of transparency in public financial management and the absence of effective accountability mechanisms have enabled corruption to thrive in the DRC.

The failure to punish those responsible for embezzlement has also perpetuated these practices.

3. Future Perspectives

The future of financial Machiavellianism in the DRC depends on the country's ability to address institutional challenges and implement comprehensive reforms.

Strengthening Institutions

Combating financial Machiavellianism requires strengthening governance institutions in the DRC. This includes creating more robust mechanisms for oversight and transparency, as well as strictly enforcing anti-corruption laws.

Promoting Transparency and Accountability

Promoting transparency in public financial management is crucial to preventing corruption. Establishing accountability mechanisms to ensure that those responsible for embezzlement face consequences is equally important.

Mobilizing Civil Society

Active participation from civil society is essential to ending financial Machiavellian practices. An engaged civil society can play a key role in monitoring government actions and holding leaders accountable.

International Cooperation

Collaboration with the international community can also aid the DRC in fighting corruption. Technical and financial support from international partners can enhance local capacities to implement effective reforms.

Conclusion

Financial Machiavellianism in the DRC is the product of decades of political instability, institutional weakness, and conflict. This chapter has shown how these factors have contributed to the apex of this phenomenon, which continues to hinder the country's development. Combating these practices requires strong political will, institutional strengthening, and active participation in civil society. Only through an integrated and inclusive approach can the DRC break from its past and build a more transparent and prosperous future.

CHAPTER 14

CONCLUSION

The journey through this book has been an in-depth exploration of the financial, governance, and systemic challenges facing The Democratic Republic of Congo (DRC). By tracing the historical roots of financial Machiavellianism, analyzing its current dynamics, and examining its impact across various domains, this work has revealed how entrenched corruption and the strategic misuse of public resources have significantly hindered the nation's progress. Yet, this narrative is not one of despair; it is a call to action, a testament to the resilience of the Congolese people, and a beacon of hope for transformative change.

The DRC's paradoxes are striking: vast natural wealth exists alongside persistent poverty; cultural diversity flourishes amid political instability; and a population rich in creativity and determination operates within a framework of weak institutions. These contradictions highlight the pressing need for systemic reforms that can break the cycle of mismanagement, inequality, and exploitation that has defined much of the country's post-independence history. Addressing these challenges is not only essential for the nation's development but also critical for restoring dignity, opportunity, and justice to its people.

Lessons from the Journey

Throughout this book, we have uncovered the complex interplay of historical, political, and economic factors that have shaped financial governance in the DRC.

We have examined how financial Machiavellianism operates, from manipulating monetary and fiscal policies to the exploitation of natural resources, and how external forces—foreign powers, global financial institutions, and multinational corporations—have influenced the trajectory of the Congolese economy. These insights are not merely a critique of past failures but also a foundation for understanding how to forge a better path forward.

The analysis has also underscored the critical role played by non-state actors, such as civil society organizations and the media, in exposing corruption and demanding accountability. Despite significant obstacles, these groups have been at the forefront of the fight for transparency and justice, demonstrating the power of grassroots movements to challenge entrenched systems of exploitation. Their work provides a model for the type of active, engaged citizenry needed to transform the DRC's future.

A Call for Action

As this book concludes, it is clear that the DRC's challenges are daunting but not insurmountable. The road to reform is paved with difficult choices, requiring political courage, social solidarity, and a collective commitment to justice and equity. To overcome the legacy of financial Machiavellianism, the DRC must undertake bold and comprehensive reforms in several key areas:

1. **Institutional Strengthening:** The foundation of any meaningful reform lies in strong, independent institutions. This includes judicial systems that can enforce laws without

fear or favor, financial oversight bodies equipped to track and prevent corruption, and governance frameworks that prioritize transparency.

Institutions must not only exist but also operate with credibility and integrity, earning the trust of the Congolese people.

2. **Economic Diversification:** The DRC's overreliance on natural resources has made its economy vulnerable to exploitation and external shocks. Diversification into sectors such as agriculture, manufacturing, renewable energy, and technology is essential to create a more resilient and inclusive economy. This shift requires strategic investments, capacity-building, and the empowerment of local entrepreneurs to drive sustainable growth.

3. **Citizen Empowerment and Participation:** Change cannot be imposed from the top down; it must be driven by the people. Civil society, grassroots movements, and ordinary citizens must be empowered to hold leaders accountable and actively participate in shaping the nation's future. Public awareness campaigns, civic education, and platforms for dialogue are crucial for fostering an engaged and informed citizenry.

4. **International Cooperation with Accountability:** The DRC cannot achieve its goals in isolation. Strategic partnerships with international stakeholders are vital for accessing the technical expertise, financial resources, and global networks needed for development. However, these partnerships must prioritize Congolese interests, ensuring that external support respects the country's sovereignty and benefits its people rather than perpetuating cycles of dependency.

5. **Ethical Leadership and Visionary Governance:** The transformation of the DRC ultimately hinges on leadership that prioritizes the collective good over personal gain. Leaders must embody integrity, transparency, and accountability, setting an example for the nation and inspiring trust among citizens. A visionary approach to governance that balances immediate needs with long-term goals unites the country around a shared mission of progress and prosperity.

A Vision for the Future

The Democratic Republic of Congo is a land of immense potential, blessed with extraordinary natural resources and a vibrant, resilient population. Its challenges, though significant, are not insurmountable. By addressing the structural, institutional, and social barriers that have held it back, the DRC can emerge as a model of transformation and resilience on the African continent.

This book envisions a Congo where resources are managed for the collective benefit of all, where governance is rooted in transparency and ethics, and where every citizen has access to opportunities for growth and prosperity. Achieving this vision will require a unified commitment to reform, resilience in the face of obstacles, and an unwavering belief in the nation's potential.

The journey will not be easy or quick. True transformation demands patience, perseverance, and collaboration. However, the rewards of this effort—economic stability, social justice, and a brighter future for generations to come—are well worth the struggle.

Final Reflections

This book is more than an analysis of financial governance in the DRC; it is a call to action. It challenges policymakers, academics, civil society, and international partners to think critically about their roles in shaping the future of the Congo. It is also a tribute to the resilience and determination of the Congolese people, who, despite systemic challenges, continue to strive for a better tomorrow.

Let this work serve as a guide and an inspiration for all who are committed to seeing the DRC rise above its past and fulfill its potential. Change is possible, but it requires collective action, moral courage, and a shared vision for the future. Together, we can transform The Democratic Republic of Congo into a nation that not only overcomes its challenges but also shines as a beacon of hope and progress for the entire world.

EPILOGUE

The journey of the Democratic Republic of the Congo has been one of immense hardship, but it is also a testament to resilience. The financial strategies that have hindered its progress are not immutable; they can be challenged, dismantled, and reimagined.

The insights within this book are a starting point, not an endpoint. They are meant to inspire deeper reflection, robust dialogue, and concerted action. The path forward requires the collective will of policymakers, citizens, and the international community to prioritize justice, equity, and sustainability.

The DRC's wealth is not merely in its minerals or forests; it lies in its people and their unyielding spirit. As we turn the page on this narrative, let us commit to a future where the nation's potential is fully realized—a future where financial decisions serve the greater good and prosperity is shared by all.

BIBLIOGRAPHY

- Machiavel, N. (1532). The Prince.

- Strange, S. (1996). The Retreat of the State: The Diffusion of Power in the World.

- Economy. Cambridge University Press.

- Ferguson, N. (2001). The Cash Nexus: Money and Power in the Modern World, 1700-2000. Basic Books.

- Nzongola-Ntalaja, G. (2002). The Congo: From Leopold to Kabila: A People's.

- History. Zed Books.

- Kanku, A. (2018).

- Collier, P., & Hoeffler, A. (2005). Resource Rents, Governance, and Conflict. Journal of Conflict Resolution, 49(4), 625-633.

- Asongu, S., & Nwachukwu, J. C. (2017). Foreign Aid and Governance in Africa. Journal of Economic Surveys, 31(5), 797-822.

- Ferguson, J. (2006). Global Shadows: Africa in the Neoliberal World Order. Duke University Press.

- Rotberg, R. I. (2009). China into Africa: Trade, Aid, and Influence. Brookings Institution Press.